she blooms softly

bobbie collins

bobbie collins

authorHOUSE

AuthorHouse™
1663 Liberty Drive
Bloomington, IN 47403
www.authorhouse.com
Phone: 1 (800) 839-8640

© 2017 bobbie collins. All rights reserved.

Illustrated by Joyce Van Dermark
Cover and author portrait by David Hahn

No part of this book may be reproduced, stored in a retrieval system, or transmitted by any means without the written permission of the author.

Published by AuthorHouse 07/25/2017

ISBN: 978-1-4389-8513-8 (sc)
ISBN: 978-1-4389-8514-5 (hc)
ISBN: 978-1-4389-8515-2 (e)

Print information available on the last page.

Any people depicted in stock imagery provided by Thinkstock are models, and such images are being used for illustrative purposes only.
Certain stock imagery © Thinkstock.

This book is printed on acid-free paper.

Because of the dynamic nature of the Internet, any web addresses or links contained in this book may have changed since publication and may no longer be valid. The views expressed in this work are solely those of the author and do not necessarily reflect the views of the publisher, and the publisher hereby disclaims any responsibility for them.

*... the risk to remain tight in a bud
was more painful
than the risk it took to blossom.*

- Anais Nin

*If we had no winter,
the spring would not be so pleasant:
if we did not sometimes taste of adversity,
prosperity would not be so welcome.*

- Anne Bradstreet

If Winter comes, can Spring be far behind?

- Percy Bysshe Shelley

she
blooms
softly

This book is dedicated to:

the wind...

The wind rustles trees, climbs the mountains
Stirs waves that pound into the land
Clears clouds from the sky, glides the birds and
Cheers flowers when they understand

- Bobbie Collins

how could i tire of its unique complexity -
the wind?

- bobbie collins

🌹 she blooms softly 🌹

prologue 1

innocence 13

turmoil 33

resolution 77

epilogue 93

i want to hug you with my words...

i want to wrap soft words
around you gently...
serene words to soothe you...
warm words to enfold you and
      hold you tightly...
in a safe and special place
inside my heart...

i want to splash bright words
upon you gently...
wise words to calm you...
vast words to stretch you and
      let you soar...
to a high and lofty spot
inside my mind...

i want to lift grand words
under you gently...
sweet words to caress you...
splendid words to inspire you and
      set you free...
with a light and secret space
inside my soul...

i want to hug you with my words...

spring 2005

prologue

prologue

she blooms softly

I started to write at age fifteen
On paper I poured out my soul
For then I had no one to share with
And thus all my words I'd inscroll.

The implement of my expression
Of thoughts that just could not be said
For always my notebook would listen
And into my verse then I fled.

T'was then I did write so profusely
Life's burdens I silently bore
But gradually opened myself, then
Wrote less as I learned to talk more.

My life's new direction is sharing
My hopes and my dreams and my fears
My thoughts and my feelings but sense that
You've turned now to me deafened ears.

I write this as if it were to you
But all that I write is for me
If you hear these words it won't matter
The writing of them sets them free.

My notebook, you see, it still listens
I know not thus yet if I'll dare
To see if you too want to hear them
These words, I know not if I'll share.

bobbie collins

    amidst the trees
    cottoned with snow
    a flower blooms
        alone
    in the hushed wilderness...
    blossoms faded
    yet radiant
        against the bleak whiteness
            of winter...
    vibrant color
        against the harsh blackness
            of naked trees.

    this flower
        audaciously
            stands not ashamedly
                but exultantly.

    fear her not.

    alone she stands
        in her incongruity
        a dichotomy...
            anomaly.

she blooms softly

ah you say
"it is not right
for such a flower
    to bloom
       in this so bitter season."

she defies you...
but fear her not.

she has conquered
      winters past...
the cold wind
      cannot chill her...
instead
she warms the air
      about her.

nothing
      can destroy her now.
she will always bloom again
for inside
      she carries
      perpetual summer.

accept her.

winter 1982

she blooms softly

*A pause in my wandering journeys
Uncharted, unknown and unplanned
I'm piecing the puzzle of my life
Together and thus understand.*

*For those who do not grasp the meaning
Of history that passes before
They are then condemned to repeat it
Again and again evermore.*

*Oh yes I have spun in life's cycle
Returning to places of old
Awareness uplifts, though, the spiral
And skyward it does then unfold.*

*Though life is a circular model
We can't change the seasons or days
Each can though reach up or plunge downward
A helical form thus arrays.*

*I'd stumble, I'd slide back and into
Abysses of life I'd descend
Each time though climb back even higher
Life's summits I'd thus comprehend.*

*My verse flows from peaks and from valleys
As pieces they are but a few
With hindsight I now fit together
The interludes which thus ensue.*

she blooms softly

no one
i
am nothing

i was
but
am no more

an ice cube
in
lemonade

a summer day

winter 1963

※ innocence ❀

she blooms softly

*The soil I was raised on was rocky
Instead of rich earth it was sand
I learned to survive without nurture
Exist without aid from the land.*

*My roots, although feeble, they served me
Found sustenance where e're they could
I learned to adapt and grew slowly
And life in the forest withstood.*

*Oh I was an innocent flower
Naïve, oh I was, full of trust
I bent with each breeze that swirled 'round me
And knew not the meaning of lust.*

*So meek and so fragile I was then
Brought low by the winds when they blew
But learned, from the willow, resilience
And that strength alone saw me through.*

*Again and again I pulled upright
Soon after each storm made me bow
And saw that the brittle had broken
So thus in my childhood did vow:*

*Through storms, I would keep my eyes open
And constantly seek out all truth
To age and yet not become bitter
But keep the sweet guile of my youth.*

bobbie collins

now... today...
      i am sixteen...
then... tomorrow...
      i am seventeen...
but... actually... i'm not really
      ...seventeen
i'll never be
      ...seventeen
for
i am sixteen
      ...plus one
      ...or two
      ...or twenty...
a world... opens... big and new
      and grown-up
      and confusing
      and (if i want) ugli
but... i can decide
i can make it
      ...chirping orioles
      ...budding roses
      ...bubbling creeks
if i want...
if...
i am sixteen
forever...
and ever...
and...

autumn 1963

she blooms softly

The flower you seek says she's taken
But hides quite a lot from my view
Though close once we now are so different
She's changed from the one that I knew.

From wild once she now has grown stately
Reserved and demure and refined
She's chosen a course that I choose not
It's not down the path that I wind.

It's sad and I grieve when it happens
When someone who once was a friend
Goes off in a different direction
And closeness thus comes to an end.

Oh yes, we may go through the motions
Of habits and simply respond
As always, but that won't diminish
The gap that has broken the bond.

When I was a young tender flower
A close friend from me did estrange
As children we had played together
But then she decided to change.

Yet I was not ready to grow up
A child I still wanted to be
I clung to the spring of my youth then
Though sad that she left without me.

bobbie collins

i like her.
she's minnehaha creek
in march...
    or april...
    or may...
swirling under bridges
thru the city
past my house.
sometimes
little boys
or big boys
or even girls
throw sticks or leaves
into the creek.
they float along...
sometimes
they get caught
going around a turn
in the creek.
and then the falls...
splashing
little drops of water
on me
if i stand
on the bridge
below.

autumn 1963

she blooms softly

once upon a time
there was a creek
in springtime
she had two names...
one was minnehaha...

we used to talk
the creek and i
about many things
that others didn't even understand.
and we played together...
i laughed...
and she laughed back at me.
we had fun together...

but then one day
she decided
she was too grown up
to travel
in her well-worn path.
so she changed her route
she went to flow with the big rivers
    -the minnesota
    -the mississippi
she left for bigger and more important things.
but she forgot one thing.
she forgot someone who missed her...
and that was me...

bobbie collins

      i walked along her abandoned banks
      i went to the falls
           minne-
           haha falls
      but they didn't laugh
      or sing...
      then i felt a splash
      but it wasn't her...
      it was warm and salty
      and it hurt
      and more splashes
      came quickly
      but little boys nor little girls live forever...
      so i dried my eyes...
      and walked away
      lonely...

      but someday
      i will go to the river
      and love it grown-up style
      and then i hope it will love me too
      grown-up style
      someday
      i hope...

      winter 1964

she blooms softly

Yet it's her pale blossom you want now
Our differences tell me of you
You want not this noisy wild flower
Unruly and vibrant in hue.

I want to be tame, in a garden
Yet let my blooms spring to and fro
And petals arrange with no pattern
And blossoms not set in a row.

Perhaps what I want is too much then
To keep all the pluck of my birth
Yet live thus in a mellow garden
And grow my roots deep in the earth.

We change, oh we change and I have too
Though part of me still is the same
I'm still the wild flower I have been
Yet over the years I've grown tame.

To be wild and tame seems contrary
Just one and not both may we be
I spent many years in confusion
In wonder of which one was me.

The botany books list the genus
And species of flowers that grow
Dichotomy is not acknowledged
Not where I fit in did I know.

bobbie collins

qu'est-ce que c'est que ça?
what is it that it is...
i love and hate
and laugh and cry
and sing and yearn and love...
who am i...
a stranger
in the world
and life...
alone without...
and lonely within...
happi-sad
like 10¢ roles
of sour cherries...
veri grown-up
yet veri immature...
i want
and yet i don't want...
but what is it
that it is...
i understand
not...
where...
why...
who...
what...
qu'est-ce que c'est que ça?

autumn 1964

she blooms softly

The wild I describe is emotion
Vivacious raw passion of youth
To cynics, maturity's lacking
Sophisticates call it uncouth.

I balanced 'tween child and adult then
As others my age did the same
But then when adulthood had won them
It all was a strange aloof game.

I could not resolve the dilemma
Of having to hide what I felt
A poker face meant I was grown-up
Not showing the cards I was dealt.

So sheltered I was in the forest
And felt not the sun from above
But timidly crept to its edges
And then did I first fall in love.

The one that I loved said he loved me
Unleashed, my emotions did flow
Until my poised friend he did meet and
To me then indifference did show.

I grieved but bounced back very quickly
And loved then again and again
But when I'd reveal my deep feelings
Away from these passions they ran.

bobbie collins

many things... i think about and wonder
and try to understand...
i love so veri much – but
what is it that i love? i think i love love...
and life... but what they are i do not
understand...
i am not alone but
alone... veri... understand... why... empty...
no tears but crying... hurt...
sobbing sobbing... pain inside...
how easy for none.. hard hard hard
understand... hard... questions unanswered...
why why why...
tired always but no sleep... veri confused...
i know a boy...
happy outside but veri sad inside...
independent outside but dependent inside...
carefree outside but caring inside...
a man outside but a boy inside...
but not completely...
hiding from others and trying
to hide from himself... but it doesn't work...
confused... mixed up... afraid...
someday it will be passed...
little boys don't live forever... they grow up...
someday... when... how... where... who... why...
i don't know at all... but... hope... love...

winter 1965

she blooms softly

There's so much about you that's special
The depth of your feelings inside
The fire of emotions that glow, but
You're constantly trying to hide.

I see that you've passions unbridled
As stallions locked up within stalls
The wild in your nature, it lives still
I've seen it in spite of your walls.

Oh I don't begrudge you your walls, though
I know about walls and their use
Survive is what all of us must do
For walls no one needs an excuse.

Emotions that are not extinguished
Though raging they must be contained
It thus was the forest I fled to
And there for a while I remained.

And so I did learn to retreat there
To hide the extents of my soul
Alone I admitted my passions
With others I used self-control.

The dark woods did serve as my walls then
Behind the tall trees did I slink
I hid midst the brush and the bushes
Alone in that peace did I think.

bobbie collins

    tonite... i sit... and think...
    of life... and love... and things...
    so many things...
    who am i... what am i... why am i...
    what am i made of...
        way down...
            deep inside...
                farther...
                    deeper...
                        no –
                            deeper yet...
    past concreteness...
    further... into an abstract world...
    one that words cannot reach...
    because... words are manmade...
    and are too material...
    unreachable... fathomless...
    so much inside... that struggles...
    fights... desperately... tries to reach...
    an outer surface... but never quite...
    succeeds...
    so much... emotion... feeling... being...
    that has no suitable... complete...
    satiating... outlet...
    someone... someone... someone...
    (who oh god who)
    must know... without... physical...
    words...

    autumn 1965

she blooms softly

*I want to go live in your garden
To let my roots grasp the rich earth
And feel the warm sun of your presence
That sparkles with laughter and mirth.*

*I know not that much of your garden
Yet glimpses enough have I seen
To recognize good soil and thus know
The nature of your lush terrene.*

*I always have been a wild flower
And staunch in the forest I've stood
Though venturing out, I'd retreat then
Into the deep peace of the wood.*

*I wanted to be a wild flower
Roots clung to the rocks of my birth
The forest was coarse but I knew it
And feared all outside of its girth.*

*Oh yes, it was dark in my hiding
But yet it was safe and secure
The trees they did shield and protect me
And taught me their strength to endure.*

*But many did want just to pick me
To pluck off my roots from my stem
I bristled sharp thorns for protection
And closed up my blossoms to them.*

bobbie collins

look at the flower
it is young, it is fresh, it is alive, so alive
but do not pick it, for it is wild
(growing among the brush in the woods)
it is beautiful to your eyes
look at it...
look at it well... and then remember
always remember
for if you pick the wild flower
and try to hold it close to you
it will wilt and then die
enjoy it for the moment
      – the precious moment
that will never be again
but do not touch it
or its beauty will end so quickly
hold it only in your memory – forever
then it shall always be beautiful
and your life shall be changed
for all beauty that we feel – and remember –
affects our lives
as we have appreciated,
and in that we have known
and in knowing we are wiser...

she blooms softly

leave the flower then
return to the garden roses
- who are happy where they are
do not return to the wild flower in the woods
(for it might not be there)
or – worse yet – oh, so much worse yet –
you will see it at a different moment
thru different eyes
and you may not feel its beauty as before
and the memory
will no longer be sweet
walk on –
      look
      see
      feel
appreciate (and thus know)
remember – yes, always remember
and then pass on
softly, quickly...

winter 1966

turmoil

she blooms softly

Alone I did hide in the forest
Beneath the strong limbs of the oak
With birches and spruce as companions
In innocence wrapped as a cloak.

But silence became desolation
It held not the comfort of old
I needed to touch and be touched by
The sun's warmth and flee from the cold.

The sun, it could scorch, yes, I know that
But I was so young and naïve
Out there was the daylight I yearned for
That dark shelter thus I did leave.

Headlong towards bright light I did run then
Away from the forest I rushed
Uncloaked, I embraced all of life, but
Exposed so, I quickly was crushed.

My blooms were flung down by a harsh world
My petals were bitterly raped
The flower I had been was beaten
My blossoms were battered and scraped.

The seasons descended upon me
No more was I sheltered by trees
Unready I was for the winter
Defeated, I fell to my knees.

bobbie collins

you listened
- and understood
and in understanding
...you cared
you cared enough
enough to put aside
your own desires
for something
that meant so much
so veri veri much...
god help me!
      please...
we shared one nite
a moment of our lives
we shared
and in sharing understood...
and now i disappear...
a thousand years from now
they'll say
"how cold she is –
how distant
      far away
she sees
but feels not, cares not, loves not
      god damn her..."
and you will hear them
but you will know
you shall remember
one nite
      shared...

she blooms softly

and you will say
"i knew her in the fall
when she was still alive
but slowly dying...
i knew her then
and understood
and cared...
but she is gone now
dead
as fall succumbs to winter...
the flower once so vital
is choked and frozen
until at last
it bows its head
     and dies."
you will find others
who will say
"i knew her in the spring
when she first began
to sing and dance and love...
when she pushed her tender sprout
above the still cold earth...
and first began to greet the dawn
and smiled and laughed and loved..."

i knew her then.

winter 1967

she blooms softly

That winter was harsh and so bitter
I thought it had frozen me too
I'd felt the cold penetrate deeply
Believing my soul's life was through.

But somehow I lived through that winter
The willow had taught me quite well:
Be supple, not brittle (I learned) and
Survive thus the harshest cold spell.

'Twas over a year 'til the thaw though
Until that cold winter dispelled
But once having left knew I could not
Stay long in the woods where I'd dwelled.

Trees gave me protection, for certain
But kept out the light of the day
I'd hide 'til I captured my strength back
And only 'til then could I stay.

Outside of the forest was sunshine
So that's where I wanted to grow
But now knew the fury of seasons
Fierce storms, burning heat, ice and snow.

Alone in my walls of the forest
I'd heal and not suffer from pain
But loneliness, bleak isolation
Upon my scarred soul they did reign.

bobbie collins

how do you express, share,
the feelings and emotions
that crush your whole being
between their fingers...
'til the seed pushed against the skin,
trying to break...
to release the red juicy pulp
    in a splattering...
how can man-created words
express god-created feelings?
how do you verbalize
    the anticipation of spring?
freshness, beginning, birth, life,
coldness seeming to be warmness
because of the still vivid remembrance
of colder coldness.
wind, once bitter (fight to resist it)
now blows more strongly
but this time
bears a promise of a future...
it combs through my hair,
separating each strand...
free, free – each one is free of another
no direction is dictated –
each makes its own path.
this wind...
it blows through me...
my body is no longer a mass of solid
it blocks not this wind
but welcomes it inside.

she blooms softly

this wind...
it cleanses my mind from the dirty winter
that has lasted eight centuries too long.
it screams within me...
break, break... goddamn it – break!
spill out that which craves release.
this wind...
tears fill my eyes...
happi-sad
i cannot see what confronts me.
i cannot feel that which i grasp in my hand.
i cannot hear the noise that deafens me.
i cannot live within this world.
i cannot discover the object of my search.
the sun does not shine today
grayness encompasses all –
an ugli day to most
but oh so beautiful to me.
is there no existence
    that can share this with me?
not even one other being
    that you have created?
no one but you, god?
oh please
don't let me live my life within myself
    any longer.

spring 1968

she blooms softly

*And thus this wild flower did wander
To learn of the world and its ways
I opened my blossoms to sunshine
But closed them on dark stormy days.*

*I learned then the sun's rays were wisdom
And in them of life could I know
The truth, when intense, it could burn, yet
I needed that sunshine to grow.*

*And then I did learn of the storms too
Though furies may bring driving rain
That water, it cleansed and it strengthened
Solidity thus could I gain.*

*Through both sun and rain then the wind came
Both gentle and fierce did it blow
But yet it would leave in an instant
Eluding my grasp, it would go.*

*The magic it held did entice me
But always evading my reach
I marveled at wind but knew not how
To learn of that which it did teach.*

*And thus, so world wise, so I thought then
In thinking all battles were won
I opened myself to the clear sky
And bravely went forth in the sun.*

bobbie collins

you ask if i do not understand
no – you do not know my mind
(as well as i)
you cannot see the reach
    of my understanding
you do not know that i know
i could tell you –
but why should you believe me?
you say that i have doubt
yes – it is so... but
you were not there
    when i trusted and was hurt
or you would know that a wall
(once built up)
becomes so strong
and must be dismantled
only by pushing the rocks away
(one by one)
you see the rocks remaining
if you could but know of those
    that you have already moved
("something there is that doesn't love")
you do not see the gaps
    where trust now seeps through
you came upon the flower in the winter
when all was cold and stiff
    without color
but you were witness to the spring
(le printemps beau)
when life awoke and conquered

she blooms softly

do you not see
that there are but three seasons remaining
    -spring so childishly playful and exuberant
    -summer of warmth and understanding
    -autumn with mellowness and knowledge
but winter shall never return
    freezing the mind
        engulfing the spirit
            thwarting the soul
winter is gone forever (for)
you have placed life within my hands
(so fragile)
it is so precious and
    i cherish it
i will let the seasons change –
for in newness there is challenge
(and beauty)
but skip over the winter
    except
        maybe
            perhaps
i shall allow one snow to fall
so that the knowledge of it will be renewed
    and
the rest of the cycle
    will be better loved.

summer 1968

she blooms softly

*So sure that all winters had passed then
In trust and forgetting the pain
Fresh life swirled anew 'round this flower
The entire earth her domain.*

*She saw the world had lovely gardens
This flower thus started to yearn
For one certain garden enticing
And there she did want to sojourn.*

*For such a naïve little flower
Who wanted a sheltering sun
The garden she saw as a refuge
And so towards its soil she did run.*

*This yearning must be a progression
It can't be against nature's plan
For flowers that grew in the forest
To want to grow close to a man?*

*It cannot, it must not oppose it
The nature that won't be defiled
For t'was in the very beginning
That all of the flowers were wild.*

*So boldly but with trepidation
In springtime with skies of soft blue
This wild flower entered a garden
That promised of sunshine and dew.*

bobbie collins

he
has brushed away the tears of the child
to see the color of my eyes
he has raised her from my smallness
into a sandbox world
    of castles, paths and dreams
he has painted the sky
    with feathers and clouds...

spring 1969

she blooms softly

so free...
    free to think
    free to feel
    free to breathe
as free as spring...
    the wind
    the wild flower
    the prisoner
free not from without
but from within
free from yourself
    (is a bird really free from the sky?)
blow wind... grow flower... fly bird...
and self
    yes
    self
free me...

spring 1969

she blooms softly

That garden spoke nothing but kindness
Yet drastically changed on one day
It turned on this flower so tender
And springtime reneged me in May.

Because of a vow that was promised
The joy was then taken away
For now I was just a possession
And must thus my master obey.

My duty was only to serve him
My life was then no longer mine
He showed off his property proudly
And bragged of his flower so fine.

A flower I had been but was now
(I realized in bitter dismay)
A feather to wear in the cap of
An arrogant harsh popinjay.

I cried and I begged him to hear me
He silenced my pleas in his rage
He thought he had purchased this flower
Heartbroken, I fled from his cage.

I cynically scorned then all gardens
Deluded by love, I did flirt
And lived in the fields and the roadsides
Withholding my roots from the dirt.

bobbie collins

      i am the winter beautiful
          ...but cold
      trees nakedly dying
      strong but too strong
      brittle they do not bend
      youth of spring is past
      gnarled age uncovered by
      the deadened leaves
      icen wind penetrates even the bark skin
          in a warmless sun.

she blooms softly

snow silently covers the barren
and quiets the earth
silence reigns
    as death
all anguished screams are strangled
a shell – a mask to camouflage the ugliness
beautiful but cold
false beauty
one step and the white is blackened
    see the ugli?
look beneath the shell that hides me
blk/wht contrast – no color
i cry it:
    "spring is dead"
never to exist again
i know
i am the winter beautiful.
so veri cold.

winter 1970

she blooms softly

Denying my soul to myself then
On hills and in valleys I played
I'll love not, I'll care not, I taunted
But knew it was all a charade.

I saw in your eyes you were hurting
Yet I must have misunderstood
For men, they are rocks, like the mountains
And wouldn't feel pain if they could.

It's women, you see, who are tender
They're delicate, fragile and meek
With vulnerability flaunted
And tears that are proof they are weak.

So men who are claimed by their brethren
As children are taught crying's wrong
They must show they're sturdy and stalwart
And let the world know that they're strong.

But why that it is I do wonder
If feelings we're able to hide
The masks that we wear are our strengths and
It matters not what's felt inside.

Yet I couldn't stay in those confines
In roles of what I was to be
Though flighty I was on the outside
Inside I was able to see.

bobbie collins

life –
i have much
    to say to you...
to look – and really see
that's you
that's what you're made of
it's where you're really at

suddenly
i can see you
    -with unclothed vision
and you're truly beautiful
thru real and honest eyes

to discover
that which already was
but was not perceived
    previously
that is your beauty
and i feel you
deeply

she blooms softly

so continue
to give to me
and i'll try to reciprocate
in thanks.

autumn 1970

she blooms softly

*One day you did tell me that you were
Not easy to live with, not you
You need not have told me, I saw that
Another such wind once I knew.*

*Oh yes, you're the wind, read these pages
I wrote them a decade ago
Oh that wind was fair-haired and blue-eyed
And in my heart that wind did blow.*

*But now these same words are about you
For winds and some words, there's no time
That limits or binds their existence
For constancy tests the sublime.*

*Oh, after ten years I could write more
On winds and their value and worth
And how they bring joy to this flower
Who misses them so in their dearth.*

*There's much in this world to be cherished
The trees and the mountains, the sea
The sky and the birds and the flowers
But wind is so special to me.*

*The wind rustles trees, climbs the mountains
Stirs waves that pound into the land
Clears clouds from the sky, glides the birds and
Cheers flowers when they understand.*

bobbie collins

oh – the wind
sometimes gentle
or maybe fierce, even bitter
you can never depend on it
so ever-changing
soft or penetrating or swirling or steady
no sameness; no monotony.
never try to hold it – you can't
but play with it when it surrounds you
and grab on as it passes by
ride along for a while
drifting
yet never let it take you so strongly
or completely
or so far that you can't return
for it knows no path
and may hurl you aside,
crushing you in its wake
if you watch not carefully.
shield yourself for protection when it's cold
but open freely in its warmth
let it sway you not enough to lose your step.
you can hope for it
to bring relief in the very heat
but never plan
on the self-willed wind
for disappointment is too severe.

she blooms softly

just enjoy it as it comes and goes
ever traveling to something new
and when it is silent do not yearn
for so much beauty is always present
just place its memory
in a quiet spot within your mind,,,
only memories are kept forever
and it's our power to select
for happiness or destruction
(if goodness must be lasting to be good
then goodness does not exist)
treasure the wind for what it is
and appreciate its worth
yet realize its limits.
feel it
but you can never touch it
accept it but with open eyes
then it can only bring you joy
or help you further in your journeys
expect not more than what it can give

how could i tire of its unique complexity –
the wind?

summer 1971

she blooms softly

You see, you're the wind, as I told you
I knew that, but yet I forgot
To bask in the wind but don't ask it
To give of that which it cannot.

Such gentle a wind, but you're strong too
I leaned on that strength, yes I know
But I'd been encumbered of late and
Exhausted from that I did grow.

Oppressed from such past obligations
My weariness yoked you instead
But obviously the new burden
You bore was one I had just shed.

And thus I regret my dependence
Yet now my own power's returned
So I will move on to tomorrow
With one more new thing that I've learned.

I wish I would use all the knowledge
I gather in life as I go
I want so to touch and be touched by
So many of those that I know.

In haste I plunge clumsily forward
Intense though, I scare them away
Offending, I seem overbearing
They leave when I want them to stay.

bobbie collins

alone without
and lonely
within...
to have a friend
is to be a friend
but that is not enough.
i know when i fail
afterwards
after
when it is too late
crawl into my cave
where no one enters
no one hurts...
there i belong
i am accepted...
alone
i accept myself...
with others
i do not
because i reflect
the feelings i sense...
alone
there are not others
whose feelings are transmitted
and being perceived
hurt.
enter into my cave
(will you?)

she blooms softly

enter if you choose
stay if you choose
but leave if...
thus it is your choice
i shall not impose...
send me
an engraven invitation.
without it
i do not know.
perceptive
sensitive
insecure
so goddamn
    perceptive
    sensitive
    insecure
too goddamn...
goddamn.
give of myself
no –
others –
come and take
for i know not how to give
i am afraid to give
for i feel my gift
would be naught
and unaccepted.

winter 1972

she blooms softly

*So now you are shuttered aloofly
Unreachable, distant, withdrawn
You entered my life for a moment
And touched me, but now you have gone.*

*Accepting I am now and knowing
That some things are not meant to be
Although I'm still crazy about you
I know you do not yearn for me.*

*But that doesn't rock my foundation
Serenity's mine come what may
I used to be lost and so needy
I chased every person away.*

*My spirit was seeking and searching
My questioning plagued me no end
I wanted substantial connections
But alienated each friend.*

*I wandered my days at this juncture
Without a life plan to arrange
But I was so totally clueless
Distractedly hunting for change.*

*My life was composed and unruffled
No trauma perched outside my door
But hunger inside had me longing
Some part of me wanted much more.*

bobbie collins

    i want something but
        i know not what it is.
    when i find it (if i do)
        it will come from inside of me
        but i can't find anything else
            inside of me now
i'm always so much alone
        even when i'm with people
i reject them
why?
am i so unique?
certainly every woman
        is an entity unto herself –
yet others can reach out to people
        –or do they?
why am i so different?
maybe i'm not –
maybe i just don't see inside of others
        like i see myself.
i wonder what it would be like
        to be somebody else.
it seems contradictory
        that in order to live with myself
        i cannot live with others.

she blooms softly

i want to be alone
      only by process of elimination
        - i don't want to be with anyone else.
does one necessarily exclude the other?
i'm not unhappy
    but i'm not happy either.
content with myself
      but discontent
      with my alienation from others
i want to escape
      because i don't see a solution
but to where?

how can i judge myself objectively
when i am subjective unto myself?

winter 1973

she blooms softly

*As far back as I can remember
(The first time I cannot recall)
Each year I would battle depression
The episodes recurred each fall.*

*It's now called "affective disorder"
When "seasonal" they call it "SAD"
In those days I knew of no label
Describing the feelings I had.*

*Each autumn descended upon me
With leaves turning golden and brown
I called it "my annual depression"
For I was incredibly down.*

*But then I'd grow numb in the new year
Though frozen, such hope it would bring
For knowing my soul would awaken
When winter did melt into spring.*

*Because I could see my life's cycle
Would follow the seasons each year
My hope turned to stark desperation
One spring when the message was clear.*

*I could not discard this depression
It lingered to burden my soul
I felt I was futilely clawing
But trapped in a sinister hole.*

bobbie collins

    i am so sad inside
    and so very empty...
    it's warm outside
    but that warmth
        won't reach inside of me.
    i used to be exuberant
    what happened to me
        inside?
    why cannot this spring penetrate?
    was my joy only naivety?
    has bitterness
        killed
        the happiness
            inside?
    has knowledge
        made me see
        the emptiness?
    has winter
        descended
        so coldly
        as to freeze
            the roots of me?
    why does the spring
        not breathe
        the warmth of life
            back into me?
    where is the sun?
    do i want too much... to thusly
        be satisfied with nothing?

she blooms softly

i hate the world
because of what it caused me
    to do to myself
i built a wall of ice
that will not thaw
what am i going to do
    with myself?
i stay so far away from people
but crave closeness.
but i'm so afraid...
each time i venture out
...it hurts
i cause my own misery.
my idealism
    keeps getting slapped down
    by reality.
maybe it's not good to try
    to look at the world as it exists.
is ignorance the only bliss?
i reach out
    to touch the world
    and want it to touch me
        in return.
perhaps my touch is
    so icen
    that it
    doesn't prompt a response?

spring 1975

resolution

Introduction

she blooms softly

I saw no escape from my gloom, so
Despondent and hopelessly bleak
With glaringly strong trepidation
"Professional help" I did seek.

He wanted me on "medication"
I argued that "drugs" weren't for me
I'd face all my demons clear headed
Thank you; but insistent was he.

Explaining that bones which have broken
For healing they needed a "cast"
I called them a "crutch" and resisted
But then I surrendered at last.

Once numbed, to my utter amazement
Intense and profound dialog
Cut through the entrenched desolation
I suddenly saw through the smog.

I found that the core of my being
Concluded that I had no worth
My logic rejected such insults
I wasn't that way at my birth!

Awareness dispensed with my searching
Unneeded, I soon ceased my pill
Since now with my pathway cemented
My struggles were focused uphill.

bobbie collins

    the world is nowhere
       - i cannot touch it.
    it is a stranger to me
      and i to it.
    i am suspended
      in nowhere
      and with me
        the world has stopped
    (i perceive yet disbelieve)
    no –
      it's still spinning
    i have merely stepped off
      and am spinning
        in my own
          minute
            sphere.

she blooms softly

today i said
   i felt small inside
   but yet could not
     explain my words
now i think
   i understand.
i need
   to touch a larger sphere
   than my own.
i think i'll sleep now
   and do that in the morning.

summer 1975

she blooms softly

*The dawn brought the rays of the sunshine
Its warmth chased away all the fear
And suddenly I did awaken
To realize the sun was that sphere.*

*Though deep in the forest I lingered
This time it exploded in song
Of joy and supreme exultation
I found what was there all along.*

*Though I did grow small in the forest
Compared to the tall leafy trees
I learned from their wizened green branches
That rustled and swayed in the breeze:*

*To reach up and stretch myself skyward
Don't settle for less than my fill
Hang on to my dreams, be they lofty
Believe they'll come true and they will.*

*I reached and found plenty of sunshine
Abiding in forest so deep
The wind parted leaves and the sun's rays
Thus into the dark woods did seep.*

*I learned then that all which I yearn for
Is there if I want to but see
I'll cling to my hopes and continue
To look for a garden for me.*

bobbie collins

a new spring
awakens into mellowness and serenity
wrapping me within its arms
of gentle sunshine
in harmony with the warmth
    inside to
defy past winters of angry blizzards
and icen walls...
    i am not afraid of tomorrow
    for i have known yesterday
    and i love today.

dawn discards the darkness
to impart understanding
with the wisdom
    of the sun.

she blooms softly

youthful exuberance
gives way to quiet happiness
as comprehension conquers fear
and eyes now seeing
eagerly perceive another
                turning...
with comfort (and security)
of a new knowledge
to welcome openly
        this
            spring.

spring 1976

she blooms softly

*T'was then I did find a new garden
That beckoned me into its arms
The warmth of its sun was so gentle
And I was beguiled by its charms.*

*Entranced I was barely aware that
So closely to it I did creep
Until I stood full in that garden
And silently sunk my roots deep.*

*Thus nurtured and warmed by the sunshine
Into a deep slumber I slipped
But gradually wakened my eyes to
Discover myself in a crypt.*

*In sleeping my roots had stretched downward
Not seeing the vine overhead
Which covered that once lovely garden
Its growth by my blossoms was fed.*

*Its density blocked out the suns rays
On my tender stems it did coil
To suffocate, strangle and starve me
The nutrients sucked from the soil.*

*The sweetness still lured, but to save me
I struggled and pulled myself free
My soul's inner strength will not suckle
The universe solely owns me.*

bobbie collins

softly
    she blooms softly

gently
    she screams gently

touch her
    with the warmth of knowing sunshine

she cries laughingly

(magnolias heavy the air)

she blooms softly
    brazenly

brush her
    with the cool of laughing breezes

she blooms softly

the silent noise
    thunders quietly
    unbridled
    gently

she screams gently

sweep her
    with the colors of fiery seas

caress her
    softly

embrace her
    gently

she yearns for
    the garden of the wind

softly, gently

summer 1982

epilogue

she blooms softly

*The years have gone by in a flurry
But wasn't it eons ago
When I was so fragile, so troubled
And knew not the things I now know?*

*I traversed the highs and the lows then
So anguished, I tried to find me
I had not the wisdom I have now
For I was unable to see:*

*Oh I was just one struggling human
A mixture of strong traits and weak
The same as all others, yet special
Because of my talents unique.*

*So after my stumbling striving
To sort it all out in my head
I finally found a clear vision
And chose a firm pathway instead.*

*The life I've been living is steady
And filled with an inner strong peace
But my obligations have ended
And now I flow free with release.*

*I'm thrilled my new chapter is starting
Allowing my reach towards my goal
Pursuing the wind's luscious garden
Fulfilling the depths of my soul.*

bobbie collins

then... and now...
different... and the same...

the outside is the same...
the world still spins round...
the sun shines, the rain rains...
the wind still blows...

the inside is the same...
the soul still reaches out...
the emotions feel, the thoughts think...
the words still flow...

the grounding is different...

then the flower lived upon a sea...
with the waves,
always the waves...
calm, still, some days...
up heaving others...

now the flower lives in a house...
roots captured in a clay pot...
a house without enough windows...

old doors are opening...
new doors are opening...
she peeks out...
and beholds the spring...

she blooms softly

springtime is special for a flower...
she blooms in the sunshine...
her roots soak up the rain...
she dances in the wind...

when she is outside...

but she is inside...
looking outside...
yearning...

she aches to be free...
free to let her roots
grow deep into the rich earth...
free to be bathed
with warm sun and cool rain upon her face...

free to feel the wind...

spring 2005

she blooms softly

*The sphere that is me is a blossom
Which basks in the warmth of the sun
My stem is my strength of resilience
To steady each day that's begun.*

*New sprouts and new petals both grant me
Awareness; with dawn they unfold
To drink in the sphere of the sun, which
Is knowledge and wisdom untold.*

*The sphere of the earth is my home, but
Where on it I live is my choice
Terrains and the climates are lifestyles
The options are mine, I rejoice.*

*My roots are security, keeping
My soul safe from rages above
They reach ever down through the earth, for
The nutrients there are but love.*

*Relationships are my life's gardens
I want such to never rescind
The rich soil of love, that I always
Might dwell in a garden of wind.*

*With love flowers bloom so profusely
Their vibrant rich colors unfurled
For flowers, you see, they bring beauty
To all of the rest of the world.*

bobbie collins

she knows
she understands
she accepts
she surrenders

the wind chooses
the wind always chooses
    its own path

for that is
    the way of the wind
    the essence of the wind
    the nature of the wind
    the splendor of the wind

she blooms softly

she knows
    that to pick a flower
    removes all sustenance
    and the flower dies

she understands
    that to capture wind
    and place it in a bottle
    makes it air, not wind

she accepts
    differences between flowers and wind
    flowers share radiant blossoms
    wind soars to breathtaking heights

she surrenders
    to the sun rising in the east
    to the river flowing downstream
    to the wind in its chosen path

she knows
    the way of the wind
she understands
    the essence of the wind
she accepts
    the nature of the wind
she surrenders to
    the splendor of the wind

she loves

summer 2005

About the Author

Unrequited love moves some to despair... but may move artists to create.

So began the author's journey to write, in precise trimeter quatrain rhyme, what evolved into her autobiography. Thus transcribing her epic narrative for her own catharsis, her words languished... hidden for a third of a century.

In an "aha moment", she finally realized writing was her passion. Timidly, she started sharing her words with a few friends. Encouraged by their responses, she initiated the process of completing and compiling her previous work.

Never before published, the author now offers her words to reach through to the souls of "kindred spirits".

Retired, the author currently spends "the good months" on the North Shore of Lake Superior. When views of the Big Lake cannot compensate for winters-that-refuse-to-end, she resides in North Texas, with sojourns in western Nevada, and visits to friends and relatives... plus other journeys... to many states with mild climes.

Writing poetry when the muse inspires, the author is now most prolific with her blogging. She wrote a series of essays some years ago, describing herself as "middle aged, middle class, middle-of-the-road, middle child (can't we all just get along?)".

Now relishing every senior discount, the author embraces the role of curmudgeon, to inscribe an opinion on any of the numerous and eclectic topics which interest her.

About the Artists

The pen and ink stipple illustrations were done one dot at a time by Joyce Van Dermark, a graphic designer who studied art at the Chicago Art Institute. She has taught college art classes and practiced art for many years in Dallas, TX. Her travels around the world give her inspiration for her artistic creations. In addition to drawing in ink, she paints with acrylics, makes her own greeting cards and sews quilts of her own designs.

Cover and portrait artist David Hahn created visual art throughout his career. Educated in St Louis, MO, and at Washington University School of Fine Arts, he began employment as a technical illustrator. Relocating with his wife, Virginia, to Minneapolis, MN, he expressed his artistic talents in advertising and design. Moving to Hovland, MN, in 2001, he is now "retired" as a fine artist, focusing on drawing portraits and using watercolors to share the beauty which surrounds. He also teaches art at the local K-12 (as a foster grandparent) and youth classes at the Grand Marais Art Colony.

www.shebloomssoftly.com